THE GOD WHO IS MORE THAN ENOUGH

EL SHADDAI

KENNETH E. HAGIN

FAITH LIBRARY PUBLICATIONS

Unless otherwise indicated, all Scripture quotations in this volume are from the *King James Version* of the Bible.

Fourteenth Printing 1998

ISBN 0-89276-401-5

In the U.S. write:
Kenneth Hagin Ministries
P.O. Box 50126
Tulsa, OK 74150-0126

In Canada write:
Kenneth Hagin Ministries
P.O. Box 335, Station D
Etobicoke (Toronto), Ontario
Canada, M9A 4X3

Contents

Chapter 1
The God Who Is More Than Enough

*Because he hath set his love upon me, therefore
will I deliver him: I will set him on high, because
he hath known my name.*

*He shall call upon me, and I will answer him: I
will be with him in trouble; I will deliver him,
and honour him.*

*WITH LONG LIFE WILL I SATISFY HIM, and
shew him my salvation [deliverance].*

—Psalm 91:14-16

*And when Abram was ninety years old and nine,
the Lord appeared to Abram, and said unto him, I
am the Almighty God; walk before me, and be
thou perfect.*

—Genesis 17:1

When the Lord God appeared to Abram, what He
actually said in Hebrew was, "I am El Shaddai .... "

El Shaddai is one of seven covenant names through
which God revealed Himself to Israel. In Hebrew, *El
Shaddai* means "the All-Sufficient One," or "the God who
is more than enough."

The translators of the King James Version translated
El Shaddai as "Almighty God." I like that. If He is the
All-Sufficient One, then He is Almighty: the One who is
more than enough.

All through the Old Testament, Almighty God
revealed and unveiled Himself as the God who is more
than enough.

1

He is the God of Abraham, Isaac, and Jacob. He said to Abraham, *"thy seed shall be a stranger in a land that is not theirs, and shall serve them; and they shall afflict them four hundred years; And also that nation, whom they shall serve, will I judge: and afterward shall they come out with great substance"* (Gen. 15:13,14).

Four hundred and thirty years went by. God came on the scene and spoke to a man by the name of Moses, who led the children of Israel out of Egypt.

As they were leaving, however, Pharoah's heart was hardened. He went after them with his soldiers, intending to recapture them and make them his slaves again.

The children of Israel stood on the shore of the Red Sea crying, "What are we going to do? What are we going to do?" The Egyptians were behind them, and the Red Sea was before them. On one side of them was wilderness, and on the other side were mountains.

The God who is more than enough spoke to Moses and said, "Stretch forth thy rod." When Moses did so, the waters of the Red Sea parted long enough for the children of Israel to go across on dry ground. They were delivered!

When the Egyptian army attempted to follow, they were drowned in the depths of the sea.

A modernistic preacher wrote, "Well, really, that wasn't much of a miracle. The water was only *ankle deep* at the place they forded."

When I read that, I thought, *Dear Lord! That poor simpleton thinks a whole army drowned in ankle-deep water! It would have been a greater miracle than ever for a whole army to drown in ankle-deep water!*

The issue is not that they drowned in ankle-deep water; the issue is that God divided the waters and Israel crossed over dryshod. It happened just like the Bible says it happened: God divided the Red Sea.

When the children of Israel arrived safely on the other side, the women got out their musical instruments and began to sing and dance. In the song the Spirit of God gave them, it said, *"the depths were CONGEALED in the heart of the sea"* (Exod. 15:8).

"Congealed" water is frozen water. God made the water stand up on both sides like a wall. He froze it. The children of Israel walked across the sea on dry ground. The Word was spoken, and the water came together again. **He's more than enough!**

Once the children of Israel had reached Canaan's land, they ran into other difficulties. One day they were fighting a crucial battle against their enemies. It was getting dark. If night fell, they might lose the battle. Joshua, their leader, prayed that the sun and moon stand still in the sky (Joshua 10:13).

And God stopped the whole universe because a man of God prayed! God could do that because He is the Almighty God—the All-Sufficient One—**the God who is more than enough!**

All through the Old Testament, we see this God who is more than enough revealing Himself in the lives of men and women: patriarchs, prophets, priests, and kings.

We see Elijah praying on Mount Carmel and the fire of God falling from heaven to consume the sacrifice. The prophets of Baal were defeated (1 Kings 18). **He's the God who is more than enough!**

We see David's mighty men of war and think we are reading the exploits of supermen. Although they did supernatural feats, they themselves were not wounded or killed. They overcame their enemies because the power of God was upon them. **He's the God who is more than**

enough, even in the midst of war!

Coming over to the New Testament, we see Jesus appear on the scene and declare, *"he that hath seen me hath seen the Father"* (John 14:9). He told the Jews, *"Your father Abraham rejoiced to see my day: and he saw it, and was glad"* (John 8:56).

They answered, *"Thou art not yet fifty years old, and hast thou seen Abraham?"* (v. 57).

Jesus said, *"Before Abraham was, I am"* (v. 58).

God had revealed Himself to Moses in the Old Testament as the great God I AM. Jesus was trying to tell the Jews, "I am that God. You are looking at God right now." The Lord Jesus Christ demonstrated in His earth walk that He is the great God I AM. **He is more than enough!**

We see Jesus and the disciples out in the wilderness with the multitude. This was the occasion He preached what we call "The Sermon on the Mount." The people had been without food for several days and were almost fainting from hunger. Jesus told His disciples to give the multitude food to eat.

They replied, "We don't have anything!"

They looked around and all they found was a little boy who offered them his lunch: five barley loaves and two small fish (John 6:9).

Jesus had them seat the crowd in groups. He took the little boy's lunch and fed the 5,000. **He's more than enough!**

A famous modernist preacher said, "Well, that's really no miracle. After all, the loaves of bread were *bigger* in that day than they are today."

He was forgetting that was just *one* little boy's lunch!

When Jesus comes on the scene, He is more than

enough!

We see Jesus attending a wedding in Cana of Galilee with His mother. She told Him they had run out of wine, and she instructed the servants, *"Whatsoever he saith unto you, do it"* (John 2:5).

Jesus told them to fill the water pots with water and carry them to the governor of the feast. By the time they got there, the water had been turned into wine, and the governor exclaimed, "You've saved the best till last!" **He's more than enough!**

We see Jesus approaching the city of Nain and finding a funeral procession coming out of the gates, bound for the cemetery. The dead man was the only son of a widow. So Jesus, **the One who is more than enough,** stopped the procession, walked up to the coffin, and commanded the fellow to get up. He did, and Jesus restored him to his mother. **He's more than enough!**

Word came to Jesus one day that His friend, Lazarus, was dying, but Jesus purposely tarried a few more days before making His way to Bethany.

When Martha learned that He was coming, she ran out to meet him, saying, "Oh, Master, if only You had been here, Lazarus would not have died!"

He said, "Your brother shall rise again."

Martha replied, "Oh, we know that he will rise again in the resurrection at the last day."

Jesus said, "I am the resurrection and the life." Then He said, "Take Me to his sepulchre."

Lazarus' body had been placed in a cave which was sealed with a stone.

When Jesus ordered them to roll away the stone, they protested. "Oh," they said, "by this time he stinks!" But they did what He asked.

Jesus said, "Lazarus, come forth!" Lazarus came forth, still wrapped and bound in graveclothes. Jesus said, "Loose him and let him go."

The God who is more than enough is greater than death!

Outside Jericho one day, Jesus saw a blind beggar named Bartimaeus sitting by the side of the road. When Bartimaeus heard that Jesus of Nazareth was approaching, he began to cry out, *"Jesus, thou son of David, have mercy on me!"* (Mark 10:47).

Jesus stopped and said, *"What wilt thou that I should do unto thee?"* And Bartimaeus said, *"Lord, that I might receive my sight."*

And, blessed be God, **He was more than enough!**

So often we want to delegate everything to the past. We say, "Oh, it was wonderful back there. God could do all those things back there. Isn't that wonderful?"

Or we want to skip over the present and talk about what it will be like when we all get to Heaven. "Someday it'll all be over," we say. "One of these days, I'm going to leave this vale of tears. Here I wander like a beggar through the heat and cold . . . . "

Things can be different NOW if we'll believe God. Things will be different HERE if we'll trust Him. **He's the God who IS more than enough.**

He IS the All-Sufficient One. He is not just the God of yesterday; He's the God of NOW. He didn't say, "I'm the God who WAS more than enough." No! He didn't say, "I'm the God who WILL BE more than enough." He said, "I AM El Shaddai."

Because it was in the divine plan of God, Jesus took upon Himself our sins and our diseases. He put Himself into the hands of sinful man, was nailed to the cross, and gave up the ghost.

Jesus couldn't be killed until He was made sin for us. He took our place. He had to go down into the prison house of death for us, because He was our substitute.

I can imagine that all the devils of hell raced up and down the back alleys of hell rejoicing, "We've defeated God's purpose!"

But on that third morning, the God who is more than enough said, "It is enough! He has satisfied the claims of Justice."

Death is of the enemy. The Word of God says that until Jesus was raised from the dead, Satan had the power of death.

But Jesus conquered death. Down in hell He put off from Himself the principalities and the powers, making an open show of them, triumphing over them in it (Col. 2:15). [He later told John on the Isle of Patmos, *"I am he that liveth, and was dead; and, behold, I am alive for evermore; and have the keys of hell and of death"* (Rev. 1:18).]

As He ascended, He went by the tomb and got His body.

Mary, arriving at the tomb intending to finish the embalming process, found His body gone. "Where have they laid Him?" she asked a man she supposed to be the gardener.

When He answered, Mary realized it was Jesus the risen Lord. She reached out to touch Him.

He said, *"Touch me not; for I am not yet ascended to my Father: but go to my brethren, and say unto them, I ascend unto my Father, and your Father, and to my God, and your God"* (John 20:17).

When He ascended on high, Jesus entered into the heavenly Holy of Holies with His own blood to offer as an eternal sacrifice for us.

Then He returned to earth and said to His disciples, "Peace be unto you."

They were frightened. "It's a spirit," they cried.

Jesus replied, *"Behold my hands and my feet, that it is I myself: handle me, and see: for a spirit hath not flesh and bones as ye see me have"* (Luke 24:39).

He had already offered His own precious blood on high. Now they could touch Him.

Thank God, He is the Almighty God. He is the All-Sufficient One. **He is the God who is more than enough.**

Chapter 2
Seven Things God Wants To Do for You

In the 91st Psalm, there are seven things *El Shaddai*—the God who is more than enough—said He will do for the person who sets his love upon Him:

"Because he hath set his love upon me, therefore will I

(1) DELIVER HIM:

(2) I will SET HIM ON HIGH, because he hath known my name.

(3) He shall call upon me, and I WILL ANSWER HIM:

(4) I WILL BE WITH HIM in trouble; I will deliver him,

(5) and HONOUR HIM.

(6) WITH LONG LIFE WILL I SATISFY HIM, and

(7) SHEW HIM MY SALVATION."

We need to understand the importance of the simple phrase "I will" or "I shall."

A very learned man once addressed a group of us ministerial students. This man had an excellent working knowledge of many languages. In fact, when one of the students asked him how many languages he was fluent in, he replied, "thirty-two."

This scholar was a translator for the U.S. Government during World War I. He was recognized as the leading Hebrew and Greek scholar of his day.

The day he visited us, he was sitting reading his Greek New Testament. He said, "There are some things in the Greek—and this would be true in some cases in the Hebrew—for which we have no idiom in the English language.

"For instance," he said, "here in John's Gospel the 14th

chapter and the 13th verse, where Jesus said, '*whatsoever ye shall ask in my name, that will I do,*' the King James Version says, '*I will.*' "

He went on to explain, "Now, the translators felt they ought to use either 'I will' or 'I shall,' because that is the strongest assertion you can make in the English language. You can't say anything stronger than 'I will do it,' or 'I shall do it.' The translators thought they should make it the strongest assertion that can be made in English."

The scholar read the verse to us in the original Greek (it was all Greek to me). Then he said, "Now I'm going to translate that literally for you."

This is what it *literally* says:

"If you will ask anything in My Name, if I don't have it, *I'll make it for you*"!

"I'll make it for you"! And, thank God, He can. Because He is *El Shaddai*—**the God who is more than enough!**

I was reminded of this incident because in the 91st Psalm God says "I will do" the following seven things.

First: "I will DELIVER HIM."

Thank God, this God who is more than enough is a delivering God!

As we saw earlier, He told Abraham his descendants would be sojourners in a foreign land for 400 years, but He promised, "I will bring them out with a strong hand."

God doesn't forget His promises: 430 years after their captivity began in Egypt, God raised up Moses and Aaron to lead Israel out of bondage—and He brought them out with a strong hand. He's still the same delivering God today! **He is more than enough!**

According to Acts 10:38, "*God anointed Jesus of Nazareth with the Holy Ghost and with power: who went about doing good, and healing ALL that were oppressed of the devil; for God was with him."*

Satan is the oppressor. Jesus is the Deliverer.

Second: "I will SET HIM ON HIGH, because he hath known my name."

This point will be studied with the fifth point.

Third: "He shall call upon me, and I WILL ANSWER HIM."

God always has been a prayer-answering God. All through the Bible, God said, "I will answer."

Jeremiah 33:3 says, *"Call unto me, and I will answer thee, and shew thee great and mighty things, which thou knowest not."*

In Isaiah 43:25,26, God said, *"I, even I, am he that blotteth out thy transgressions for mine own sake, and will not remember thy sins."* Then he added, *"Put me in remembrance . . . . "* (v. 26).

Remind Him of His promises! Remind Him of His Word!

Coming over to the New Testament, we find marvelous promises that thrill our hearts:

> **MATTHEW 7:7,8**
> **7** Ask, and it shall be given you; seek, and ye shall find; knock, and it shall be opened unto you:
> **8** For every one that asketh receiveth; and he that seeketh findeth; and to him that knocketh it shall be opened.

> **MARK 11:24**
> **24** Therefore I say unto you, What things soever ye desire, when ye pray, believe that ye receive them, and ye shall have them.

> **JOHN 16:23**
> **23** And in that day ye shall ask me nothing. Verily, verily, I say unto you, Whatsoever ye shall ask the Father in my name, he will give it you.

Coming to the Acts of the Apostles, we see that He is still a God who hears and answers prayer; **a God who is more than enough.**

One day Peter and John were on their way into the Temple through the Gate Beautiful when they saw a man, lame from birth, begging alms. It was at the hour of prayer, 3 o'clock in the afternoon.

The Bible says that Peter, "fastening his eyes upon him," said, "Look on us." The man looked up, expecting to receive some coins. But Peter said, *"Silver and gold have I none; but such as I have give I thee: In the name of Jesus Christ of Nazareth rise up and walk"* (Acts 3:6).

As Peter took the beggar by the hand and lifted him to his feet, his feet and ankle bones became strong. He was healed immediately, and he accompanied them inside the Temple area, *"walking, and leaping, and praising God"* (v. 8).

When news of this miracle spread, a crowd gathered. Peter and John were arrested for preaching, and the next day the chief priests and elders commanded them to preach and teach no more in the Name of Jesus (Acts 4:18).

"And being let go, they went to their own company, and reported all that the chief priests and elders had said unto them" (v. 23). Bless God, I like that! They went to their own company.

Then the whole company of believers lifted up their voices together in prayer to God and said, *"now, Lord, behold their threatenings . . . ."* (v. 29). They concluded their prayer by saying, *"grant unto thy servants, that with all boldness they may speak thy word, By stretching forth thine hand to heal; and that signs and wonders may be done by the name of thy holy child Jesus"* (vv. 29,30).

The Bible says that the place where they were

assembled was shaken, and they were all filled with the Holy Spirit (v. 31). Bless God, we need some praying like that today—praying that will shake the very places where we're praying.

He's a prayer-answering God. He said, *"I will answer him."*

Another example is found in the 16th chapter of Acts, where we find Paul and Silas in jail at Philippi.

They are in the innermost prison. Their feet are in stocks, and their backs are bleeding, because they were beaten. *"And at midnight Paul and Silas prayed, and sang praises unto God: and the prisoners heard them"* (v. 25).

At midnight! It literally happened at midnight! But there is also a symbolic thought here. In the midnight of your life — in your darkest hour — the Bible tells you what to do. At midnight they prayed and sang praises to God.

The fact that the other prisoners heard them means they didn't do it silently; they did it out loud. Yes, the prisoners heard them, but somebody else heard them, too—**this God who is more than enough!**

I can just see Him looking down over the banisters of heaven and asking one of the angels, "What in the world is that noise?"

The angel reports, "That's Paul and Silas down there in jail."

So God reaches over the banisters of heaven, as it were, takes hold of that jail, and shakes it until every door flies open, every window flies open, and every cell door flies open.

The jailer, seeing this, thinks the prisoners have escaped. Knowing their escape would cost him his life, he is preparing to fall on his sword and kill himself when Paul said, *"Do thyself no harm: for we are all here."*

The jailer called for a light, sprang into their cell, and fell trembling before Paul and Silas, asking, *"Sirs, what must I do to be saved?"*

They replied, *"Believe on the Lord Jesus Christ, and thou shalt be saved, and thy house"* (v. 31).

He was saved that very night, and they had a midnight supper at his home.

Looking at the Epistles, the Apostle Paul said:

PHILIPPIANS 4:6
6 Be careful for nothing; but in every thing by prayer and supplication with thanksgiving let your requests be made known unto God.

The expression *"Be careful for nothing . . . . "* is not too clear. A better translation is, "Do not fret or have any anxiety about anything."

God doesn't want you to worry or be anxious about a thing. If you are, you shouldn't be. He said, *"Be careful for nothing."* Why? Because He's the God who is more than enough: the All-Sufficient One, the One who never changes, the One who never fails. He is just as able today as He ever was. (Jesus Christ is the same yesterday, today, and forever.) And He's interested in *you.* He's concerned about *you.* That's why He said, *"Because he hath set his love upon me, therefore . . . I will answer him."* He didn't say, "If it's my will, I will answer him." He said, *"because he hath set his love upon me, I will answer him."*

If your love is set upon God, your will is in line with the Word of God. A man or woman walking in fellowship with God will never ask anything outside of the will of God. And *the Word of God is the will of God.*

Fourth: "I WILL BE WITH HIM in trouble; I will deliver him."

God didn't say you weren't going to have any trouble just because you've been born again and filled with the Spirit. In fact, He rather infers that you are going to have trouble *because* you're a Christian.

The world is going to persecute you. They're going to talk about you. They're going to speak evil of you. And the devil, who is the god of this world, will put pressure on you at every turn.

When this happens, some people think it's God who is putting pressure on them. No! Satan is the author of sickness and disease.

JOHN 10:10
10 The thief cometh not, but for to steal, and to kill, and to destroy: I am come that they might have life, and that they might have it more abundantly.

Here Jesus is contrasting His works with the works of the devil. God is not a thief. Jesus is not a thief. Heaven's not a thief. The devil in hell is the thief. He is called the god of this world in Second Corinthians 4:4. And he's out to defeat you.

He's walking about as a roaring lion (1 Peter 5:8). No, he's not *a* roaring lion; he is *as* one, seeking whom he may devour. And he'll devour you if you let him. But, thank God, you don't have to.

No, God didn't say we would never have any troubles, but He did say, "I will be with him in trouble."

PSALM 34:19
19 Many are the afflictions of the righteous: but the Lord delivereth him out of them all.

Half of them? No, *all* of them. This God who is more

than enough, the All-Sufficient One, delivers him out of *all* of them. In the Old Testament, this word "affliction" doesn't mean sickness and disease; the Hebrew word actually means "test" or "trial." That's what your troubles are: tests and trials.

Some people seem to be content to stay in trouble. They say, "The Lord's with me." But He's not just *with* you; He's there to deliver you! He's there to bring you out of your troubles. The troubles of the righteous are many, but the Lord delivers them OUT of them ALL.

> **JAMES 5:13,14**
> 13 Is any among you afflicted? let him pray. Is any merry? let him sing psalms.
> 14 Is any sick among you? let him call for the elders . . . .

James is talking about three different things:
Is any *afflicted?* Let him pray.
Is any *merry?* Let him sing.
Is any *sick?* Let him call for the elders of the church.

As the Word says, the afflictions of the righteous are many, but the Lord delivers him out of *all* of them, because He promised to do so. The Almighty God promised. The God who is more than enough said, "I will deliver him."

Somebody has said that the argumentative kind of prayer is the best kind, and I sometimes think it is.

The story is told about a black woman who was in trouble many years ago in the days of slavery. Her 16-year-old daughter was about to be sold on the auction block.

The mother bowed her head and prayed, "Dear Lord God, if You were in trouble as I am in trouble, and I could help You as easy as You could help me, I would do it!"

This story is a historical fact; a U.S. Senator was present. The senator's 15-year-old son was with him, and when the boy saw them pulling this girl away from her mother, and he saw their tears, he ran to his father and said, "Daddy, loan me $10!" The senator gave him the $10, and the boy ran to the auction block.

Before anybody else could start bidding, he said, "I will bid $10." (Ordinarily, $200 would have been a low opening bid, but everybody was so thrilled at what he was doing that nobody else would bid.)

The boy bought the girl for $10. Taking the bill of sale, he marched right over and handed the girl back to her momma.

God heard and answered that prayer. She had said, "If I could help You as easy as You could help me, I would do it."

I've told about that dear old black woman's prayer more than once, and I have followed her example and have gotten results.

I just say, "Lord, if You were in trouble like I'm in trouble, and I could help You as easy as You could help me, I would do it." And He does—He does! Because He says in His Word, "I will do it. I'll be with him in trouble. I will deliver the man who sets his love upon me." This God who is more than enough says, "I will answer him. I will be with him in trouble. I will deliver him."

Fifth: "I WILL HONOUR HIM."

Whom will God honor?

PSALM 24:3,4
3 Who shall ascend into the hill of the Lord? or who shall stand in his holy place?
4 He that hath clean hands, and a pure heart; who hath not lifted up his soul unto vanity, nor sworn deceitfully.

You can't cleanse your own hands, and you can't purify your own heart. But you can be cleansed by His blood and stand in the holy place, because He has cleansed you and robed you in His righteousness.

"I will honor him," God said. "I will set him on high." These are two of the seven things God said He would do for the person who has set his love on Him.

I would rather have God's honor than the greatest honor this world can bestow. The world honors politicians, statesmen, generals, educators, and scientists, but if they're going to honor any kind of a preacher, they'll honor some modernistic preacher who doesn't believe in the Virgin Birth or the authenticity of the Word of God.

The world as a whole is never going to honor a real Bible-believing, tongue-talking, divine healing-practicing preacher of the Gospel any more than they honored Jesus. No, you must compromise or back off a little and lay down the power to get this world to honor you. I would rather have God's honor.

Jesus Himself told John on the island of Patmos, *"To him that overcometh will I grant to sit with me in my throne, even as I also overcame, and am set down with my Father in his throne"* (Rev. 3:21).

History tells us that as Napoleon was reviewing his troops one day, his horse began to rear. A young buck private stepped forward, took the horse by the bit, and quieted it down.

Napoleon said, "Thank you, captain" (thus promoting him to captain immediately).

He said, "Captain of what, sir?"

Napoleon replied, "Captain of my personal guard."

So the buck private moved into the rank of captain, but all the other officers shunned him, because they had earned their rank, and his was granted to him.

Napoleon noticed this, so when he next called for a review of his army in full regalia, he rode side by side to the parade grounds with this young captain. The other officers realized he was a favorite of Napoleon's, and they began to court his favor.

The people of this world may not know it, but the time is coming when they are going to find out that we born-again, Spirit-filled, tongue-talking, divine healing-believing folks are favorites of the King of Kings and Lord of Lords, and they will wish they had courted our favor.

"I will honor Him," God said.

Chapter 3
How To Enjoy a Long Life

Sixth: "WITH LONG LIFE WILL I SATISFY HIM."

Oh, I *love* it! Not "I might"; not "maybe I'll do it"; not "perhaps it will be so." He said, "I WILL satisfy him with l-o-o-o-n-g life!" And I believe every word of it, bless God!

Somebody said, "Now, Brother Hagin, I knew a preacher, Brother So-and-so. He was a wonderful man of God, and he died at age 42."

Well, that doesn't mean I have to! I don't know what he believed, but I know what I believe—and I know that the God who is more than enough said, *"with LONG life will I satisfy him."*

No, that's not talking about *eternal* life, as so many people think. Thank God *for* eternal life. We have eternal life in our spirits right now.

Eternal life does not simply mean that I'm not going to die—that I'm going to live forever. The sinner is never going to die, either. He's going to live in one place, and we're going to live in another. We are a spirit-being, whether we're saved or unsaved.

We born-again Christians have Eternal Life—the life and nature of God, the divine nature—in us. And when we die, we'll leave this world and go to be with Jesus.

Paul, writing to the church at Philippi, said, *"For I am in a strait betwixt two, having a desire to depart, and to be with Christ; which is FAR BETTER"* (Phil. 1:23). He might have said, "It is better," but notice he says it is "*far* better."

Writing to the Corinthians, Paul said:

SECOND CORINTHIANS 4:16
16 For which cause we faint not; but though our
outward man perish, yet the inward man is renewed
day by day.

SECOND CORINTHIANS 5:1
1 For we know that if our earthly house of this
tabernacle were dissolved, we have a building of God,
an house not made with hands, eternal in the heavens.

"For we KNOW . . . . " Paul says. Not "we hope so." Not
"we guess so." Not "maybe so." We KNOW. I like that.
That fellow Paul was positive. He's my kind of preacher.
Later in the same chapter he again says "we know."

SECOND CORINTHIANS 5:6-8
6 Therefore we are always confident, KNOWING
that, whilst we are at home in the body, we are absent
from the Lord:
7 (For we walk by faith, not by sight:)
8 We are confident, I say, and willing rather to be
absent from the body, and to be present with the Lord.

What is it we know, Paul?
That while we are at home in the body, we are absent
from the Lord. We are willing to be present with the Lord,
the eighth verse says. That's where we're going to be: with
the Lord.
What about the sinner? He's going to spend eternity
somewhere, as the Lord Jesus Christ Himself said to us in
Luke:

LUKE 16:19-28
19 There was a certain rich man, which was clothed in
purple and fine linen, and fared sumptuously every
day:
20 And there was a certain beggar named Lazarus,

which was laid at his gate, full of sores,

21 And desiring to be fed with the crumbs which fell from the rich man's table: moreover the dogs came and licked his sores.

22 And it came to pass, that the beggar died, and was carried by the angels into Abraham's bosom: the rich man also died, and was buried;

23 And in hell he lift up his eyes, being in torments, and seeth Abraham afar off, and Lazarus in his bosom.

24 And he cried and said, Father Abraham, have mercy on me, and send Lazarus, that he may dip the tip of his finger in water, and cool my tongue; for I am tormented in the flame.

25 But Abraham said, Son, remember that thou in thy lifetime receivedst thy good things, and likewise Lazarus evil things: but now he is comforted, and thou art tormented.

26 And beside all this, between us and you there is a great gulf fixed; so that they which would pass from hence to you cannot; neither can they pass to us, that would come from thence.

27 Then he said, I pray thee, therefore, father, that thou wouldest send him [Lazarus] to my father's house:

28 For I have five brethren: that he may testify unto them, lest they also come into this place of torment.

This portion of Scripture is *not* a parable, as so many think.

In every parable Jesus told, He said, "So and so is *likened* unto so and so." In this passage, He didn't say so and so is *likened* to anything. He said, *"There was a CERTAIN rich man* (v. 19) *. . . and there was a CERTAIN beggar* (v. 20)."

You don't use the word "certain" in a parable, because "certain" means "for sure; this way and no other."

Jesus said there was a certain rich man. And it's certain he left this world and went down to what he called "this place of torment."

All of us are going to live somewhere in eternity: We who are born again are going to live in heaven, and sinners are going to live in hell. (Do not confuse Eternal Life with Psalm 91:16, *"With LONG life will I satisfy him."* This verse is not talking about spiritual Life in eternity; it is talking about natural long life here on this earth.)

Somebody said, "A long life is just an Old Testament blessing." No, it's not just an Old Testament blessing. He missed it by a thousand miles.

Not too long ago I was reading after a certain fellow who is supposed to be a great Bible teacher. (Everybody who is *supposed* to be a great Bible teacher isn't, and some folks who seem to think they know so much know so little.)

This fellow wrote in one of our national religious periodicals, "Long life, physical life, is not a blessing of the New Covenant. It was a blessing of the Old Covenant."

I thought to myself, *Well, it would have been better for us to have stayed back under the Old Covenant then, wouldn't it?* But no, long life is a blessing of the New Covenant, too.

I tore the magazine up. I didn't want anybody else to get hold of it.

Bless God, I know He's more than enough, because the devil almost defeated me in this very area.

I was born prematurely with a deformed heart on August 20, 1917 in McKinney, Texas. I never ran or played like other little children. I never laughed. I didn't have anything to laugh about. I was afflicted. I couldn't run or jump.

Then, when I was 15 years old, I became totally

bedfast, and the doctors said I would die. I spent 16 long months on the bed of sickness and disease. My body became almost totally paralyzed. My blood was pale orange in color.

One of my five doctors said this blood disease would prove fatal to me even without the paralysis and heart condition. I was advised, "Go down the middle of the road and stay ready to go."

Well, I *was* ready to go as far as being saved was concerned, but I didn't want to go into eternity just yet. I wanted to stay here a little longer. The desire to live is strong in the heart of the young.

I got into the Bible because my heart (or spirit) told me to. Oh, how much better off we would be if we learned to follow our spirits!

My spirit—my inward man—told me I didn't have to die; there was hope for me. I found it in God's Word.

As a 16-year-old boy, just 6 days before my 17th birthday, I prayed the prayer of faith for myself and walked off that bed of sickness.

I began to act upon that Word—Mark 11:23,24—and my paralysis disappeared like a snowball in the hot August sunshine. The blood condition was healed. And the heart was well. Blessed be God, I was healed! This happened on the second Tuesday of August 1934 in the front bedroom of 903 E. Greenville Street in the city of McKinney, Texas.

I got up and walked around my room, but I didn't tell my family. They thought I was losing my mind over the Bible as it was. They had tried to discourage me from spending so much time reading it. They had told me, "The Lord doesn't heal nowadays. All that has been done away with."

But I found out that He does heal; I believed He does; and I got healed.

I got out of bed the next day, too, and walked around the room when my family wouldn't know it. That second night, I said to my mother, "Momma, I want you to lay out my clothes. I'm going to get up in the morning and go to the breakfast table."

"Do you know what you're doing, son?" she exclaimed.

"Yes," I said. "I know what I'm doing. I'm healed. I'm well."

After much persuasion, I got her to lay out my clothes. The next morning, the third day after my healing, I got up and fully dressed myself, and I sat there in a chair in my room, waiting for time to go to breakfast.

I came from a broken home. Momma and I lived with her parents. Grandpa got up early every day and sat on the porch swing out on the porch until time for breakfast. This was in 1934.

When we heard that old porch swing squeak as he got up out of it to head for the dining room, we knew it was 7:30. We could set our watches by that squeak. It was 7:30. Grandpa ran on schedule.

I sat in my bedroom until I knew Grandpa was in the dining room. In fact, I waited until I was sure that the whole family was seated. Then I walked out of my room, across another bedroom, entered the dining room, and pulled back the chair at my place at the table.

Grandpa looked up and said, "Is Lazarus raised up? Is the dead raised?"

I said, "Yes, the Lord raised me up."

He said, "Well, ask the blessing."

So I blessed the food.

Then he said to my grandmother, "Get a plate" (for

there was no place set for me).

We sat and ate in silence. You didn't talk at Grandpa's table. Especially if you were a child or young person. Grandpa was a very unemotional fellow. He wasn't ever much of a fellow to talk.

He lived to be approximately 90. But if he were still alive today and I took you to his house and said, "Grandpa, I want you to meet Brother So-and-so," he would have said, "How do you do, sir," shaken hands with you, and sat there the rest of the day and never said another word.

When you got ready to go, he would have said, "I'm glad to meet you," and that would have been the end of it. He was just that kind of fellow.

If you were a guest and your children talked at the table, you wouldn't last long, because Grandpa would just stop eating, put his knife and fork down, and stare at you until they hushed. That gets embarrassing after a while, you know.

You didn't do much talking even as adults at Grandpa's table. Granny and Momma might have said a few words to one another, but there were no other words spoken at the table. It's amazing how fast you can eat if you don't talk so much!

I got through eating several pieces of bacon and a couple of eggs, a few good, hot biscuits, and a glass of milk. Nobody said a word. *Nobody said a word that whole breakfast*. Not one word was spoken.

After we got through eating, I got up and walked back to my bedroom. I looked at the clock. It was 10 minutes till 8. I was fully clothed, so I said to myself, *Well, I'll lie here across the bed. Momma will be in about 8 or a little after to make up the bed. When she comes in, I'll go out and sit on the porch swing with Grandpa until about 10 o'clock, and at 10 I'm going to walk uptown to the courthouse square.*

When I had been an invalid, they had let me sleep as long as I wanted. I was used to sleeping late, so I dozed off. That much exertion naturally had made me a little weak, anyway. I only weighed 89 pounds.

But suddenly I woke up. I was wide awake! At first I thought Momma had come into the room. I looked around, but couldn't see anybody. I looked at the clock (I'm a great one to look at the clock to see when things happen). It was 8 o'clock. This was the second Thursday of August 1934 in the front bedroom of 903 E. Greenville Street in the city of McKinney, Texas.

I recognized a presence in the room, but I couldn't see anybody. Then I heard a voice. To me it seemed audible.

In somber, ringing tones it said, "For what is your life? It is even a vapour, that appeareth for a little time, and then vanisheth away." There was a pause, and the voice continued, "and today thou shalt surely die." Then the voice ceased.

Supernatural? Yes.

God? No.

Every supernatural manifestation is not of God. You need to know that. If you don't know it, you'll find it out sooner or later; maybe to your sorrow.

But I didn't know it wasn't God. Thoughts were flying around in my mind faster than machine gun bullets can fly.

I knew that both of those quotations were Scripture, or part of the Scripture, at least. James had said the first (James 4:14), and the prophet of God, Isaiah, had told King Hezekiah he was going to die (2 Kings 20:1).

The devil can quote Scripture, too.

When I first had become bedfast—before I had found

out about divine healing—I would pray, "Dear Lord, when it's time for me to die, help me to know ahead of time so I'll have time to tell everybody goodbye."

I heard the voice again. The devil said to me—and I didn't know it was the devil—"Now, healing is right. You've been healed. All your family knows you've been healed. You got up and walked. Your paralysis disappeared. You sat down at the breakfast table and ate with them."

Then the devil decided he would misquote a little more Scripture. He said, "It is appointed unto men once to die, but after this the judgment. *Your* appointed time to die has come. God has moved in this supernatural way to tell you to get ready. You're going to die today."

If I had fallen for it—and I almost did—I would have died that day.

I thought God was standing right in that room talking to me!

I got up off the bed and tiptoed across the room. I sat in a chair by the window from 10 minutes after 8 in the morning until 2:30 in the afternoon, waiting to die. I had butterflies in my stomach. Not that I was scared to die, but the flesh recoils from death. *God didn't make us for death.*

Momma came in and said, "What's wrong, son?"

"Well, nothing," I said. (I thought I'd put off telling them goodbye as long as I could.)

"What's the matter?" she insisted.

"Nothing."

"Well, she said, "I can sense something is wrong with you."

"Nothing."

"Don't you feel all right?"

"I'm fine."

Lunchtime came. Momma called, "Lunch is ready! Come and eat."

I said, "No, Momma. I'm not hungry." (The very smell of the food as it wafted through the house made me sick to my stomach.)

Finally she brought a tray into my room and said, "I brought this to you." She put it on the table beside me and went to eat her own lunch. I called out, "Momma, come get this! The smell of it is making me sick."

"What's wrong with you?" she asked.

I wouldn't tell her.

Thanks be unto God for the Holy Spirit! No, I wasn't *filled* with the Spirit then, but I was *born* of the Spirit. Those are two separate experiences.

So I sat there from 8:10 a.m. until 2:30 p.m., never moving from my chair, waiting to die. Sometime between 2 and 2:30, however, on the inside of me I heard the words *"with long life will I satisfy him."*

These words just floated up from deep inside—from my spirit up to my conscious mind. I turned them over in my mind.

Then this other voice, seemingly so supernatural, came from the outside and said, "Yes, God has moved in this supernatural way to let you know this is your appointed day to die. Your appointed time to die has come."

I got to listening to that audible-sounding voice and lost the other, inward voice.

Ten minutes later, the same words came floating up on the inside of me to my mind, just like a kite or piece of paper would float in the air: *"with long life will I satisfy him."*

I turned that statement over in my mind. I didn't know

whether it was the Bible, Socrates, Plato, Shakespeare, or who.

This other voice spoke again from above. It sounded like it was coming from heaven. It said, "Well now, you see, God's moved in this supernatural way. You've had a supernatural experience. You're going to die today." Again I got to thinking about dying and missed the other. I didn't know where that voice came from at first. I didn't know everything then that I know now. (I didn't know much of anything then, to tell you the truth.)

The third time those words from Scripture came floating up from away down inside into my conscious mind: *"with long life will I satisfy him."*

Because I was born of His Spirit—because He was in my spirit—God gave those words to me. This time they were stronger, and this time I held onto them a little longer. But then I got to thinking again about the supernatural manifestation I had had out there in the realm where you can hear, see, and feel. So I decided *that* must be God. (Not always, my friends. Not always!)

So I lost it that time, too. But suddenly those words returned, even stronger. I realized they came from within me, but they were so strong I looked to see if somebody had slipped up behind my chair and had spoken out loud: *"with long life will I satisfy him."*

Without thinking, I said, right out loud, "Who said that? Who said that?"

Quick as a flash, that inward voice said, *"the 91st Psalm."* I hadn't known that. I had only read in the New Testament since I was saved as an invalid.

My Bible was laying on the floor under my chair. I hadn't looked at it all day. (The Holy Spirit will always lead you in line with the Word.) I reached under the chair,

got the Bible, and opened to the 91st Psalm. I read the
whole Psalm and got down to the end:

> **PSALM 91:14-16**
> **14** Because he hath set his love upon me, therefore will
> I deliver him: I will set him on high, because he hath
> known my name.
> **15** He shall call upon me, and I will answer him: I will
> be with him in trouble; I will deliver him, and honour
> him.
> **16** WITH LONG LIFE WILL I SATISFY HIM, and
> shew him my salvation.

The minute I read that, I became elated and uplifted!

But the old devil didn't give up easily. He was right
there, and that voice spoke again to my mind, "Now, that's
not for the church. That's in the Old Testament. That's just
for the Jews."

Did you ever hear that one? That's one the devil has
worked overtime. "That's not for us nowadays," he'll tell
us. "That's just for the Jews. That's been done away with."

Well, the devil robbed me of the joy and inspiration of
that moment because I didn't know any better. I thought,
*That's in the Old Testament. Maybe it is just for the Jews.
The Old Testament was written to them. It wasn't written to
me.*

Then another thought occurred to me: *Wait a minute!
Wait a minute. Bless God, I'll just run my reference. If I can
find anything in the New Testament on the subject of long
life, then I'll know it belongs to me under the New Covenant
as well as the Old!*

I began with the 91st Psalm and saw references to a
number of verses on long life. I saw that God had promised
us 70 or 80 years. These verses brought me over into
Proverbs. I got a lot of answers there. I saw there that God

said you could do certain things to make your life longer or shorter.

For example, I saw that the days of the wicked will be shortened.

Somebody will argue, "Well, I know somebody who lived a long time, yet he was wicked." Well he could have lived even *longer* without being that way. Furthermore, he could have *really* lived instead of being half dead while he lived.

I saw that if there are things you can do to lengthen or shorten your days, then people are misinterpreting Hebrews 9:27 *("it is appointed unto men once to die, but after this the judgment")*.

That verse does not say you've got *an* appointed time to die and you will die at that appointed time. If you had *an* appointed time, why did God say you can lengthen or shorten your life if you do certain things?

No, you don't have *an* appointed time to die *regardless* of what you do about it. No, absolutely not! (There are many men and women who would be alive today if they had listened to God.)

Yes, we all have *the* appointment of death. (Some will not keep it, however, because when Jesus comes, they'll be caught up with Him!)

I kept following the Bible references, and they brought me over into the New Testament. I found the Spirit of God had inspired the Apostle Paul to say in Ephesians 6:

EPHESIANS 6:1-3
1 Children, obey your parents in the Lord: for this is right.
2 Honour thy father and mother; which is the first commandment with promise;
3 That it may be well with thee, and thou mayest live long on the earth.

34 *El Shaddai*

I picked up a Full Gospel periodical a few years ago and read that an outstanding Bible teacher whose preaching and teaching I always enjoyed, had said, "Long life on the earth is not a New Testament blessing. It doesn't belong to us in the Church."

(Any of us can be right in our hearts and wrong in our heads. Don't ever follow *everything* that is said by any man: teacher, prophet, preacher, or whomever. Examine his teachings in the light of the Word.)

When I read that teacher's statement, I thought to myself, *Doesn't he know that Ephesians is in the New Testament?*

Paul spoke here of "the first commandment with promise." What is the promise? *"That it may be well with thee, and thou mayest live LONG on the earth"* (v. 3).

Then I found where Peter quoted Psalm 34:12:

FIRST PETER 3:10
10 For he that will love life, and see good days, let him refrain his tongue from evil, and his lips that they speak no guile.

I got those two scriptural witnesses, jumped out of my chair with my Bible in one hand, doubled up my fist, and kicked the devil out of the room.

I said, "Mr. Devil, you get out of here! That was *you* who moved in that supernatural way, speaking in an audible voice that sounded like it was from heaven. I'm *not* going to die today! I'm *not* going to die tomorrow! That wasn't the Bible. It's not Scripture."

I shouted out loud, "I'm not going to die next week! I'm not going to die next year! I'm not going to die in the next five years! I'm not going to die in the next 10 years! I'm not going to die in the next 20 years! I'm not going to die in the next 30 years! I'm not going to die in the next 40 years! I'm not going to die in the next 50 years! I'm not going to die in the next 60 years!"

I was six days from my 17th birthday. You add 17 onto 60 and that puts me up over 70. The promise is 70 or 80 years. Don't compromise. Don't settle for anything less than 70 or 80—*and believe for ALL YOU CAN!*

You can do what you want to, but I'm going to live LONG on the earth. Hallelujah!

More than fifty years have come and gone, and I've enjoyed divine health. I tell folks that I haven't had the flu in more than fifty years. I don't believe in having the flu. I only accept things that come from Heaven — and the flu doesn't come from Heaven.

Have you ever heard of anyone having the heavenly flu? Stop and think about it. That couldn't be right. It's always *Asian* flu, *Hong Kong* flu, etc. It comes from over where the devil and false religions are reigning supreme.

Good, Spirit-filled Christians hear on the radio, see on TV, or read in the newspaper that a flu epidemic is due, and they say, "Yeah, I'll be the first to get it." And, sure enough, they are. The devil heard them say it.

I was preaching in a Full Gospel church in October 1957 when an epidemic of Asian flu hit Southern California. I picked up *The Los Angeles Times* and the headline said that 2 million people in Southern California had the Asian flu. Our attendance dropped to 40 people a night.

The pastor of a Full Gospel church (think about it: Full Gospel—that means it's supposed to be the whole Gospel) said, "Brother Hagin, aren't you afraid you will get the Asian flu?"

"No!" I said. "I don't mind telling you, I'll *never* have

the Asian flu."

And that Full Gospel pastor, with unbelief running down his face like syrup down a syrup bucket, had such *great* respect, such great reverence, for the devil, he whispered, "Brother Hagin, I'd be afraid to say anything like that!"

I said, "Why?"

He said, "Why, don't you know the devil will hear you?"

He didn't know God's the Almighty One. He didn't know He's the One who is more than enough. He thought the devil is the one who is more than enough, and he's going to put the flu on them. He just whispered—knew he was in the presence of the devil. Sure the devil was there; he had been buddying up to and bedding down with that preacher for years. Here this preacher was, whispering in the devil's presence, "Don't you know the devil will hear you?"

"Yeah," I said. "I wanted him to hear it. I said it for his benefit. He's the very dude I *wanted* to hear it!"

Don't accuse me of being unkind; I'm telling the truth. You'd be better off to stay at home and play mumblety-peg than go hear preachers like that. Life's too short. This thing is nearly over. Jesus is coming. It's too late to play religion. The Bible is so or it's not so. If it's so, let's have it. If it's not so, let's throw it away and forget about it. But I've proven for more than 50 years that it works — it works!

Chapter 4
The Man Who Couldn't Be Saved

Seventh: "I will show him my salvation."

Salvation belongs to us.

Gipsy Smith, the English evangelist, used to tell a story about a man who came to the altar in one of his London meetings. Gipsy saw others hadn't been able to help him, and the man was struggling, so he went over to talk to him.

The man said, "I can't be saved."

"Oh yes, you can," Gipsy said. He told him the biblical story of the woman taken in adultery. He told him no matter how deep in sin he was, God would save him.

The man said, "You don't understand, Brother Smith. I work in the bookkeeping department of a certain company. I've stolen 10,000 pounds over the years and covered it up. Now if I get saved, I'll have to straighten this up. My boss is a hard man. He'll have me put in the penitentiary!"

Gipsy Smith told him, "It would be better for you to be saved and spend the rest of your life in the penitentiary and go to Heaven when you die than it would be to remain unsaved and go to hell."

"That's too big a price to pay," the man said, and he left.

The next morning as Gipsy descended the staircase into the hotel lobby, he looked out the lobby windows and saw a hatless and coatless man running down the street. This man crossed the street in the middle of the block, flew through the hotel's revolving doors, looked wildly around the lobby, ran up the stairs, and threw his arms around Gipsy.

"Oh, Brother Smith," he shouted, "It's just like you said! It's just like you said! Earth has no sorrows that

Heaven cannot heal!"

The man told Gipsy his story. "Last night," he said, "I went home and couldn't sleep a wink. I laid awake all night wrestling with that thing, rolling from one side of the bed to the other. Finally I decided I'd go straighten it out this morning."

He continued, "This morning I stood outside the company president's office for 10 minutes, trying to get enough courage to go in. I would start to open the door but would back off from it. I knew he was in there. I knew he's a hard man. Finally I told myself, *You've got to do it!* I opened the door, stepped inside, and was speechless. The president said, 'Speak up, man. My time is valuable. What do you want?'

"I stepped over to his desk and said, 'I went to Gipsy Smith's meeting last night.' And the president said, 'Well, did you get saved? Everybody else who goes out there does.'

" 'No,' I told him, 'I didn't get saved. That's why I'm here.'

"The president said, 'There's no use coming to see me. I'm just an old sinner. I don't know anything about it. No use coming to see me.'

" 'But you don't understand,' I said. 'I've stolen 10,000 pounds from this company. I have to make it right. I've kept it covered up all these years. I gambled it away on the races, and I can't pay it back.' I began to weep. I said, 'I want to make Heaven, and that thing stands between me and God.'

"My employer chomped down on his cigar and said, 'I'll tell you one thing, man. I'm sending you to the penitentiary. You're the most trusted employee I had. I met with the Board of Directors just last week. They voted to promote you to that desk right over there next to my personal secretary. But now I'm going to send you to the pen.'

"I told him, 'Well, that's all right, bless God. The burden's gone now, and I'm happy. I'll just spend the rest of my days shouting in the pen.' "

The bookkeeper told Gipsy he looked up and saw his employer chomp down on his cigar again. The man said, "You know, on second thought, I believe what I'll do is promote you. You can get enough extra salary per year to pay back that 10,000 pounds with interest in several years." Then he said, "Man, just take the day off. Have a holiday. You've found God."

The bookkeeper forgot his coat and hat and ran out of that office down the street to Gipsy Smith's hotel. As he told his story, he was jumping up and down shouting. Gipsy said, "Both of us started shouting."

You see, God showed him His salvation. That salvation belongs to every sinner; to everyone out of fellowship with God—**the God who is more than enough:** El Shaddai.

ABOUT THE AUTHOR

The ministry of Kenneth E. Hagin has spanned more than 60 years since God miraculously healed him of a deformed heart and incurable blood disease at the age of 17. Today the scope of Kenneth Hagin Ministries is worldwide. The ministry's radio program, "Faith Seminar of the Air," is heard coast to coast in the U. S. and reaches more than 100 nations. Other outreaches include: *The Word of Faith*, a free monthly magazine; crusades, conducted nationwide; RHEMA Correspondence Bible School; RHEMA Bible Training Center; RHEMA Alumni Association and RHEMA Ministerial Association International; and a prison ministry.

The Word of Faith

The Word of Faith is a full-color monthly magazine with faith-building teaching articles by Rev. Kenneth E. Hagin and Rev. Kenneth Hagin Jr.

The Word of Faith also includes encouraging true-life stories of Christians overcoming circumstances through God's Word, and information on the various outreaches of Kenneth Hagin Ministries and RHEMA Bible Church.

To receive a free subscription to *The Word of Faith*, call:

1-888-28-FAITH — Offer #603

(1-888-283-2484)

**To use our Internet address:
http://www.rhema.org**

RHEMA
Bible Training Center

Providing Skilled Laborers for the End-Time Harvest!

Do you desire —

- to find and effectively fulfill God's plan for your life?
- to know how to "rightly divide the Word of truth"?
- to learn how to follow and flow with the Spirit of God?
- to run your God-given race with excellence and integrity?
- to become not only a laborer but a *skilled* laborer?

If so, then RHEMA Bible Training Center is here for you!

For a free video and full-color catalog, call:

1-888-28-FAITH — Offer #602
(1-888-283-2484)

To use our Internet address:
http://www.rhema.org